Disability PRIDE

Accessibility Matters

Renée Marien

PowerKiDS press

Published in 2025 by The Rosen Publishing Group, Inc.
2544 Clinton Street, Buffalo, NY 14224

Editor: Michele Suchomel-Casey
Book Design: Leslie Taylor

Photo Credits: Cover AnnGaysorn/Shutterstock.com; (series background) P.siripak/Shutterstock.com; (series disability pride colors) rudall30/Shutterstock.com; p. 5 goodmoments/Shutterstock.com, (flag sidebar) Maxim Studio/Shutterstock.com; p. 7 Jovanmandic/iStockphoto.com; p. 9 Reshetnikov_art/Shutterstock.com; p. 10 JL Jahn/Shutterstock.com; p. 11 ClarkandCompany/iStockphoto.com; p. 13 Timur Malazoniia/Shutterstock.com; p. 15 peakSTOCK/iStockphoto.com; p. 17 Prostock-studio/Shutterstock.com; p. 18 Los Angeles Times; restored by User:Rhododendrites/Wiki Commons_File:Helen Keller circa 1920 - restored.jpg; p. 19 Inclusionforall/Wiki Commons_File:Malvika Iyer at the United Nations.jpg; p. 21 SolStock/iStockphoto.com.

Cataloging-in-Publication Data

Names: Marien, Renée.
Title: Accessibility matters / Renée Marien.
Description: Buffalo, NY : PowerKids Press, 2025. | Series: Disability pride | Includes glossary and index.
Identifiers: ISBN 9781499446715 (pbk.) | ISBN 9781499446722 (library bound) | ISBN 9781499446739 (ebook)
Subjects: LCSH: People with disabilities--Juvenile literature. | People with disabilities--Social conditions--Juvenile literature. | People with disabilities--Civil rights--Juvenile literature.
Classification: LCC HV1568.M375 2025 | DDC 362.4--dc23

Manufactured in the United States of America

Some of the images in this book illustrate individuals who are models. The depictions do not imply actual situations or events.

CPSIA Compliance Information: Batch #CSPK25. For Further Information contact Rosen Publishing at 1-800-237-9932.

Contents

What Is Accessibility?

Have you ever used an elevator or wheeled a suitcase up a ramp? Then you've benefited from accessibility! A space or experience is accessible when it is built to be easier for different types of people to use. For something to be fully accessible, many types of disabilities and differences must be considered, including movement, learning style, sight, hearing, age, and height.

Accessibility is important for **physical** spaces as well as **digital** ones, such as websites and **apps**. Accessibility helps people with disabilities access the same spaces as those who don't have disabilities, and it makes life better for everyone.

The disability pride flag was created to show acceptance and respect for people who have disabilities. Each color is for a different type of disability.

- The gray background is in honor of those who've died.
- Green is for disabilities that have to do with the senses.
- Blue is for those that have to with the mind and emotions.
- White stands for unseen disabilities, as well as those that haven't been diagnosed, or found out.
- Gold is for neurodiversity.
- Red is for other disabilities of the body.

Accessibility is all about making sure all people have access to the same spaces and resources as others. Offering drinking fountains at different heights makes it easier for everyone to take a drink!

Accessibility and Language

Considering people with disabilities is an important part of accessibility. The words you use when referring to both topics are important to think about. For starters, while the word "handicapped" is still commonly used with parking and bathrooms, we recommend you use "accessible" instead!

The Centers for Disease Control and Prevention says that disability is a natural part of life. Although people may not mean to be unkind, the words and phrases they use to talk about disability can be hurtful. Learn more in the "For More Information" section at the end of the book.

Learn More

As **culture** changes and we learn more about accessibility, the words we should use may change as well, and that's a good thing! If you're unsure about what to say, look it up or ask a trusted adult.

In some places, like a doctor's office, the words used can make an extra impact. If you have a disability, it can make all the difference when you're talked to respectfully.

Accessibility Rules

Most people agree that accessibility is a good idea. However, some people think it is expensive and time-consuming, so laws like the Americans with Disabilities Act (ADA) exist in the United States.

Among other requirements, this law states that when new spaces are built, doors must be a certain width for people who use a wheelchair, emergency alarms must be loud enough to alert people with hearing loss but not too loud to cause harm, and no objects can block people with vision **impairments** from using a cane.

While the ADA doesn't cover all areas of accessibility, it makes sure that many basic standards are met.

When someone who is blind or visually impaired uses a white cane, they can get a lot of information about their surroundings to help them **navigate** independently.

Learn More

When constructing a new building, including accessible features makes up less than 1 percent of total costs and allows that space to include so many more people!

Getting Around

Features that help people move around illustrate accessibility in action. Here are just a few examples:

- Doors that open with a button help people who find it difficult to open a door due to strength issues.
- Public seats, such as benches, help people take breaks when needed.
- Ramps and wide doorways help people who use wheelchairs or walkers navigate independently.

Learn More

About 13 percent of Americans identify as having a disability (most commonly affecting the ability to walk and/or climb stairs). That's a lot of people who can't enter non-accessible spaces.

- Signs with accessibility **symbols** indicate that a space will be easier to move around.

These help people who are older or have **permanent** disabilities as well as those who are hurt. They even help caregivers pushing a stroller or wheelchair!

When a space that is usually not very accessible, like a hiking trail, has an accessible feature, like a walkway or ramp, it can make a big difference to a wheelchair user.

The Power of a Sign

Let's think about the importance of signs. For example, when you go to a store, how do you know where to enter or whether a door is **manual** or opens on its own?

If there are signs that are accessible to you, imagine if they were taken away. How would you find the restroom or know how much something costs?

When we are in unfamiliar places, signs help us understand what to do and where we can go. Pictures, large writing, contrasting colors, and braille (a language that can be understood through touch) can be game changers!

Without signs that include braille, it can be difficult for someone who is blind to find the right restroom.

Accessibility Technology

Creative new ways to make life easier for people with accessibility needs are invented every day. One way is through apps available on smartphones and tablets.

Apps have been created to:

- navigate a website using only the movement of your eyes (example: Hawkeye Access)
- **caption** phone calls in real time so people who have difficulty hearing can understand the conversation (example: InnoCaption)
- take photos with a few touches and use artificial intelligence to describe what is in the photo (example: TapTapSee)

Even common messaging and notes apps can help people who are deaf or have speech disabilities communicate.

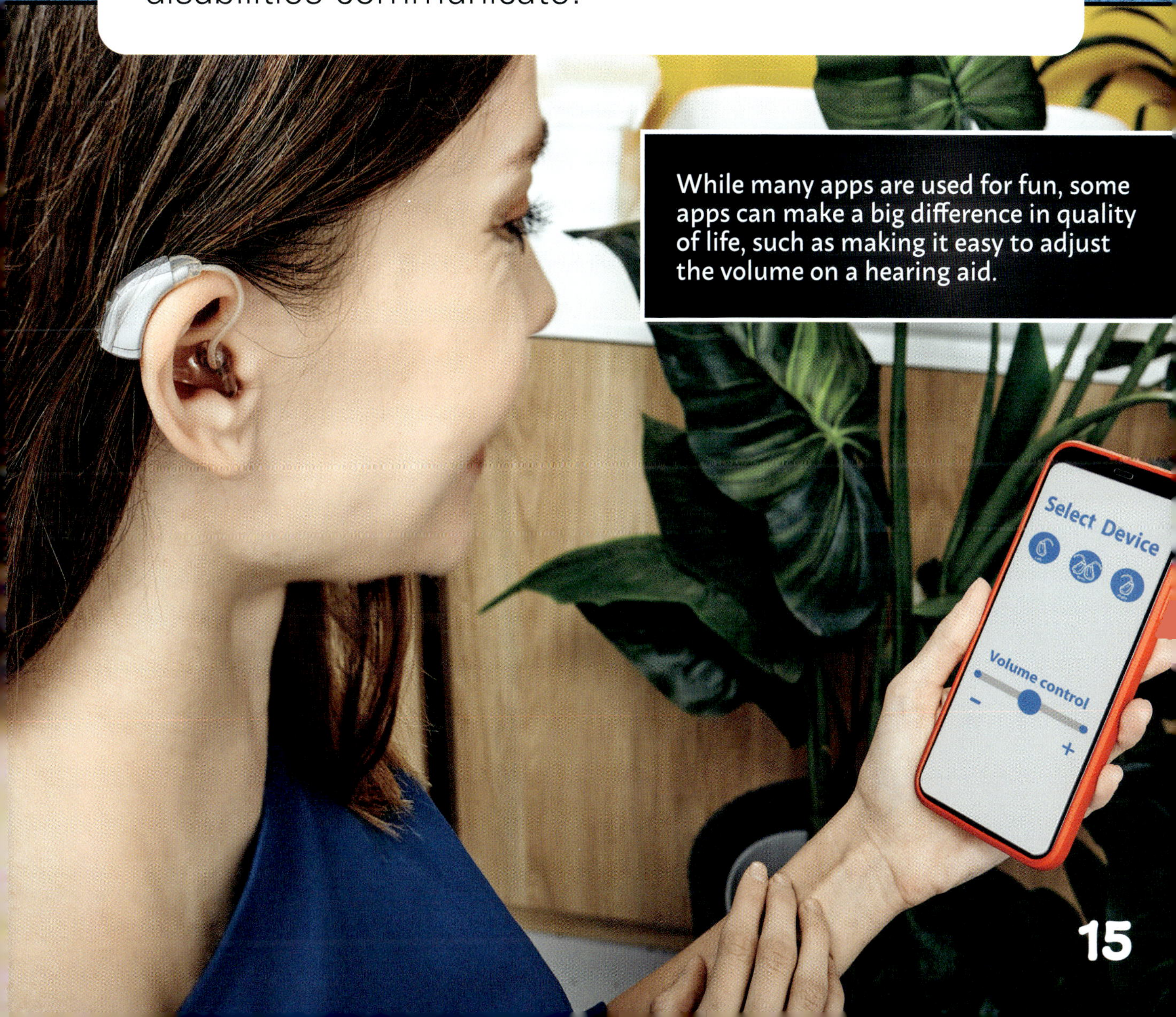

While many apps are used for fun, some apps can make a big difference in quality of life, such as making it easy to adjust the volume on a hearing aid.

Accessibility on Screens

Much of our time is spent in front of screens like computers, tablets, and smartphones. While many people use sight, hearing, and touch when interacting with these devices, there are ways to help people who cannot use these senses to use the devices too.

- Sight: Computer settings adjust colors for people with color blindness.
- Hearing: Captions can be added to videos, so what is being spoken can be read instead.
- Touch: Keyboards can be adapted to be used in different ways. They can be made larger or smaller, or can be used with head, finger, and foot movements, or even with breath!

Modern technology allows us to control our experience in front of screens. Try playing around with the settings on your computer or phone!

Learn More

Color blindness is a visual impairment in which colors are seen differently. Commonly, it makes it difficult to tell apart certain groups of colors, such as reds and greens.

Accessibility Leaders

Accessibility has come a long way because of many people who, individually or as a group, raised awareness and support for changes to be made so more people could be included in all sorts of spaces.

- Helen Keller spoke all over the world about accessibility in education.
- Malvika Iyer, a social worker, motivational speaker, and **amputee**, **advocates** for **inclusive** policies—she even models accessible clothing!

Before inspiring people around the world, Helen Keller spent a lot of time studying and learning. Think about ways that you can use what you know about accessibility to inspire others!

Malvika Iyer, shown here, has found creative ways to raise awareness for accessibility—through fashion! What other areas can you think of where better accessibility is needed?

- The National Organization on Disability helps employers make **accommodations** for people with disabilities so they can work.

Remember that advocating can be done in big and small ways. Consider things that could be more accessible in your home or classroom.

Accessibility and You

Historically, it has most often been people with disabilities who have had to advocate for the changes they needed to interact with the same spaces as others. Now we know that encouraging accessibility should be important to everyone.

Especially as technology advances rapidly, we must take responsibility in making sure that people are not left behind because of a disability or another type of difference. We must also be open to adapt and change as we learn more about accessibility to make sure that everyone knows that they are important and belong.

If you don't have a disability, it can be easy to overlook the challenges of people who do. Think about creative ways to include people in experiences by making changes and offering help.

Glossary

accommodation: Something that is supplied to meet someone's needs.

advocate: To argue for or support a cause or policy.

amputee: A person who no longer has a part of their body, like an arm or a leg.

app: Short for "application," a program that performs a task for which a smartphone or computer is used.

caption: Words that appear at the bottom of a video that describe what would otherwise be heard.

culture: The beliefs and ways of life of a certain group of people.

digital: Describes things that you interact with via a screen.

impairment: When someone has difficulty with one of their senses, such as seeing or hearing.

inclusive: Acting in a way that makes sure everyone feels included and valued.

manual: Doing something using your body rather than with technology.

navigate: To find one's way around or move through something.

permanent: Lasting for a very long time or forever.

physical: Relating to the body instead of the mind.

symbol: An object or picture that stands for something else.

For More Information

BOOKS

Brown, Keah. *Sam's Super Seats*. New York, NY: Kokila, 2022.

London, Martha. *Louis Braille*. Mendota Heights, MN: North Star Editions, 2019.

Sotomayer, Sonia. *Just Ask! Be Different, Be Brave, Be You*. New York, NY: Philomel Books, 2019.

WEBSITES

Apps for Accessibility
apps.apple.com/us/story/id1266441335
Browse through Apple's selection of accessible apps to see the new technology that exists to help people with disabilities!

Inclusion and Accessibility
youth.gov/youth-topics/inclusion-and-accessibility
This website summarizes many of the key topics about accessibility as well as provides resources on how to talk about disability and accessibility.

Youth as Self Advocates
familyvoices.org/yasa/
Read about this diverse network of teens and young adults with disabilities who are raising awareness and advocating for policies to include people with disabilities and health care needs.

Index